Werewolves

Rebecca Rissman

Raintree

www.raintreepublishers.co.uk
Visit our website to find out
more information about
Raintree books.

To order:
☎ Phone 0845 6044371
🖷 Fax +44 (0) 1865 312263
🖳 Email myorders@raintreepublishers.co.uk

Customers from outside the UK please telephone +44 1865 312262

Raintree is an imprint of Capstone Global Library
Limited, a company incorporated in England and
Wales having its registered office at 7 Pilgrim Street,
London, EC4V 6LB – Registered company number:
6695582

Edited by Adrian Vigliano, Rebecca Rissman,
  and Nancy Dickmann
Designed by Joanna Hinton Malivoire
Levelling by Jeanne Clidas
Original illustrations by Christian Slade
Original illustrations © Capstone Global Library
Picture research by Elizabeth Alexander
Production by Victoria Fitzgerald
Originated by Capstone Global Library
Printed and bound in China by CTPS

ISBN 978 1 4062 1647 9 (hardback)
14 13 12 11 10
10 9 8 7 6 5 4 3 2 1

British Library Cataloguing in Publication Data
Rissman, Rebecca.
Werewolves. -- (Mythical creatures)
398.4'5-dc22
A full catalogue record for this book is available from
the British Library.

Acknowledgements
We would like to thank the following for permission
to reproduce photographs: © 2010. Digital Image
Museum Associates/LACMA/Art Resource NY/Scala,
Florence p. **17**; Alamy pp. **11** (© Mary Evans Picture
Library), **28** (© Deco); Corbis pp. **9** (© Tim Davis),
16 (© Christie's Images), **22** (© Paul Souders)
25 (© Bettmann); FLPA p. **20** (Michael Durham/
Minden Pictures), Getty Images pp. **19** (Mike Hill/
Photographer's Choice), **29** (Redferns); Photolibrary
p. **21 left** (Jean-Michel Leligny/Photononstop);
Shutterstock pp. **10** (© Dewitt), **13** (© Fribus
Ekaterina), **15** (© Zurijeta), **18** (© David Dohnal),
21 right (© Yury Asotov).

Every effort has been made to contact copyright
holders of material reproduced in this book. Any
omissions will be rectified in subsequent printings if
notice is given to the publisher.

Some words are shown in bold, **like this**. You can find
out what they mean by looking in the glossary.

Contents

What is a mythical creature?

A **myth** is a story that has been told many times throughout history. Some myths tell us about strange creatures. Can these **mythical** creatures be real?

DID YOU KNOW?

People tell stories about dragons all over the world. Do you think dragons are real?

If you haven't seen a unicorn, does that mean they don't exist?

Shape-shifters

Many **myths** tell about creatures that change from humans to animals. They are often called **shape-shifters**. Werewolves are some of the scariest shape-shifters. They change from humans to hungry wolves!

What makes humans change into wolves?

Here are a few explanations:

- seeing the **full moon**
- wearing special clothes
- being bitten by a werewolf.

The werewolf myth

People have told stories about werewolves all over the world. The stories can be very different. But most stories tell us that werewolves are dangerous and hungry!

In some stories people are surprised when they turn into a werewolf.

Werewolf stories tell us that any ordinary person could become a hungry monster!

Werewolves in Europe

Germans tell a **myth** about a creature called the Böxenwolf (say *box-en-voolf*). It is a human who puts on a special belt to become a werewolf. The Böxenwolf is terrible and cruel.

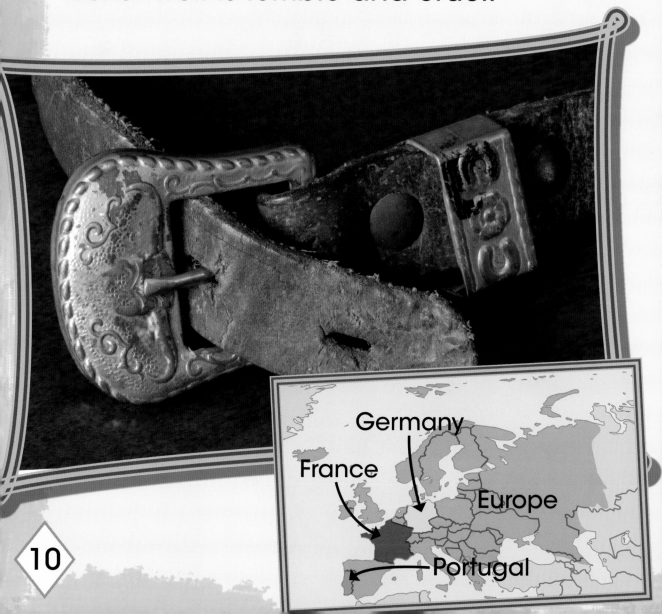

Germany

France

Europe

Portugal

DID YOU KNOW?

Stories say the Böxenwolf can be lazy. It is known for surprising travellers on the road and asking to be carried!

There are many werewolf **myths** in France. One myth is about a creature called the Louléerou (say *loo-lay-roo*). The Louléerou is a human who becomes a werewolf during the **full moon**.

full moon

DID YOU KNOW?
Once the Louléerou becomes a werewolf, it runs through the night, eating every animal in sight – even humans!

Not all werewolves are **ferocious**! In Portugal, people tell stories about a werewolf who is very sad. The lobis-homems (say *low-bis-ho-mems*) is created though a special **spell**. Once someone has become a lobis-homems, he or she spends the nights howling in the woods.

lobis-homems

DID YOU KNOW?

The lobis-homems is easy to spot. It always has a tail with short, yellow fur. But you might not see it on a dark path in the woods!

Shape-shifters in Asia

kitsune

Japanese **myths** tell about **shape-shifters** called kitsune (say *kit-soo-nay*). Kitsune are special foxes that can become humans. When a kitsune has stopped pretending to be human, it becomes a fox again.

DID YOU KNOW?

You might have spotted a kitsune if you see:

- a person with a fox tail
- a person with a fox-shaped shadow.

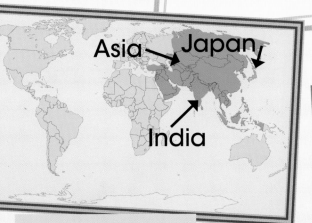

Asia → Japan
India

This is Rakshasa (say *rock-shah-sah*), a shape-shifter from myths in India.

Rakshasa

Werewolves in North America

Some North American werewolf **myths** may come from the Navajo (say *na-va-ho*), a tribe of Native Americans. The Navajo people tell stories about the skinwalkers. These are powerful witches who can change into animals.

← North America

DID YOU KNOW?

Skinwalkers can become any kind of animal they want. But they usually become coyotes, wolves, foxes, or owls.

coyote

Some Mexicans tell stories of a creature called tlahuelpuchi (say *tell-ah-poo-chee*). They are witches who turn into coyotes at night. These coyotes sneak into homes and drink the blood of human children.

DID YOU KNOW?

If you want to keep tlahuelpuchi away, you could:

- leave a mirror next to the bed
- leave a knife or scissors next to the bed.

Werewolves in Australia

In Australia, people tell stories about a mysterious **shape-shifter**. It looks like a human until a sandstorm begins. After the storm covers it with sand, the creature becomes a **ferocious** wolf!

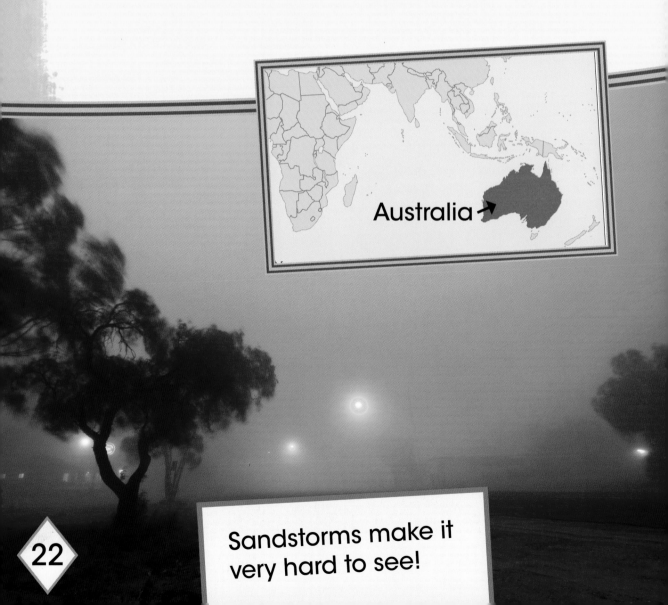

Australia

Sandstorms make it very hard to see!

DID YOU KNOW?

This mysterious sandstorm creature is sometimes called the Devil-Dog.

Close relatives

Werewolves aren't the only dangerous **shape-shifters** that are famous. Another well-known **mythical** creature that changes form is the vampire. This creature comes out at night to suck the blood of humans and animals alike!

vampire

Could werewolves exist?

 They could be real...

- People all over the world tell similar stories about **shape-shifters.**

 I'm not so sure...

- Many stories are told for fun! Just because these stories are popular, doesn't mean they're true.

They could be real...

- If werewolves can look like normal humans, they could be everywhere! We may never know who is a shape-shifter and who isn't!

 I'm not so sure...

- Nobody has actually seen a person shape-shift into a werewolf.

There are many interesting stories about werewolves. What do you think?

Reality versus myth

Wolf (real)

Found: in North America, Greenland, Europe, Asia

Eats: deer, caribou, wild boar, some small animals

Seen: in the wild, at the zoo, in photographs

Likes: hunting, sleeping, caring for young.

Werewolf (myth)

Found: all over the world

Eats: people, most other animals

Seen: in films and in stories

Likes: frightening travellers, tearing out of clothing, howling at the moon.

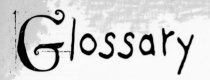

Glossary

ferocious especially frightening and powerful

full moon the moon when it is entirely lit up by the Sun. A full moon looks like a big, white circle.

myth a story that has been told many times but is not true

mythical found in myths

shape-shifter a creature that changes from one form to another. Werewolves shape-shift from human to wolf.

spell words that have magical power when spoken. Myths tell that some werewolves were created when people said certain spells out loud.

Find out more

Books

The Dark Side: Werewolves and Other Shapeshifters, Anita Ganeri (Wayland 2010)

The Usborne Book of Myths and Legends, Gill Doherty (Usborne Publishing, 2006)

Twilight, Stephanie Meyer (Atom, 2007)

Websites

http://www.wolf.org/wolves/learn/justkids/kids.asp
Learn all about real wolves at this International Wolf Centre website. It includes articles, activities, and games.

www.fieldmuseum.org/mythiccreatures/index.html
Learn about more mythical creatures at the Field Museum's Mythic Creatures Exhibit website.

Index